We Go

by Margaret Ahn
illustrated by Meryl Henderson

Pre-Decodable 13

McGraw Hill Education

Bothell, WA • Chicago, IL • Columbus, OH • New York, NY

MHEonline.com

Send all inquiries to:
McGraw-Hill Education
8787 Orion Place
Columbus, OH 43240

ISBN: 978-0-02-144848-7
MHID: 0-02-144848-5

Printed in China

9 10 11 12 13 DSS 28 27 26 25 24

We go  the  .

up ladder

We go  the 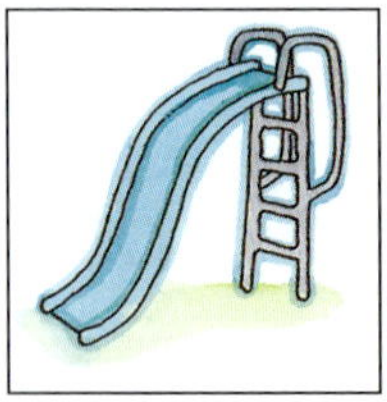.

down

slide

We go  the .

up steps

We go  the 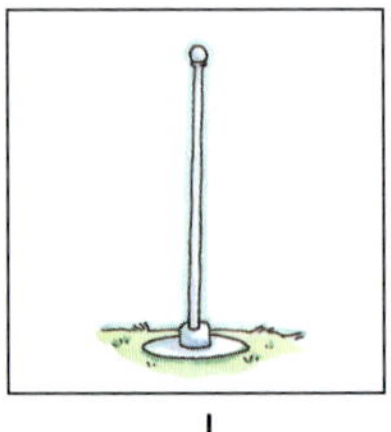.

down pole

We go  the .

up

hill

We go  the .

down

hill